SCRAPBOOKING MANUAL FOR BEGINNERS

An Essential Guide On
Everything You Need To
Know About Scrapbooking
And Tips On How To Master
The Craft Of Scrapbooking
Even As A Beginner

CW01507792

COLE ELIZABETH

Table of Contents

CHAPTER ONE

What Exactly Is Scrapbooking?

Scrapbooking is a fun and creative craft that allows you to keep precious memories, keepsakes and mementos, and channel your inner artist. Even in our fast-paced digital era, creating your own personalized scrapbook album is a popular means of preserving memories. DIY scrapbooking has gained popularity among hobbyists and crafters, transforming what was once a private pastime into an exciting and sophisticated communal event. With the growing number of online scrapbooking stores, this multibillion-dollar industry is almost certainly here to stay, even in our fast-paced digital era.

Don't worry if you've never attempted to make one. Simply keep reading to learn more about how to construct your own scrapbook. We have suggestions for where to find resources, and you may learn how to choose appropriate scrapbooking components such as high-quality scrapbook paper, pens, decorations, and so on.

What are the most well-known scrapbooking tools and materials? How do you even get started on your first album? And what are some scrapbooking ideas and techniques that you might try as a beginner?

History Of Scrapbooking

It was once returned in the 1800s, when the term "scrap book" was first used. It was once characterized as "a book with clean pages for pasting objects into." However, in fifteenth-century England, common books and friendship albums were thought to be the origins of scrap books. Guests who were invited to someone's home were requested to sign the homeowner's "friendship album" with their title and a private message - similar to the contemporary yearbook. Some pals became creative with their messages, leaving poems, quips, and even paintings. Common albums, on the other hand, are for people who want to keep their "scraps" such as letters, recipes, poems, quotes, and so on. It is similar to a photo album today, except containing keepsakes and mementos instead of photographs.

The interest has evolved over time from an easy way to keep scraps to a depiction of a student's day-today living. When photographs were no longer available, female university students wanted to be creative with their own scrapbook by using ephemera and memorabilia - from class schedules and examination booklets to a playbill, a ticket stub, and a crew of journeying cards.

With the advent of modern photography, simple remembrance scrapbooks evolved into photograph scrapbooks. What was formerly a more concerned and helpful manner of storing one's experiences and memories had evolved into something more visible and aesthetically beautiful.

The recession that followed World War I hampered the hobby's growing popularity. There was a sharp reduction in album production, and people preferred to save their ephemera, photos, clippings, and other souvenirs in a box. Photo albums have also grown in popularity over memory scrapbooks.

- Scrapbooking in the Modern Era

In 1980, a teenager from Elk Ridge, Utah, decided to preserve her family's memories by making pages using their images. She then arranged the pages in sheet protectors in 3-ring binders. Marielen Wadley Christensen compiled more than 50 volumes of what would become the cornerstone of modern scrapbooking. She and her husband decided to submit a how-to booklet titled "Keeping Memories Alive" after attracting interest at the World Conference on Records in 1981, and they eventually founded the world's first scrapbook shop, suitably named after their profitable booklet. The Keeping Memories Alive save is located in Elk Ridge, Utah, and is still open today.

Christensen's efforts to preserve her family's memories sparked the production and sale of scrapbooking supplies, transforming what was once a quaint hobby into a multibillion-dollar company.

- Trends and News in the Scrapbooking Industry

According to Anthony Thomas, "there have been roughly 25 million energetic scrap bookers, supported by over 3,000 scrapbooking stores" in the United States alone. Scrapbooking has also established a strong presence in innovative enterprise activities and conventions, such as AFCI's Creativities Show.

It originated as a man or woman hobby, a method for everyone to record their daily lives, similar to a journal, or to keep valuable ephemera and artifacts. In recent years, the hobby has evolved into a social event, with hobbyists (known as "scrappers" or "scrapbookers") participating in organizations, classes, conferences, retreats, and even scrapbooking cruises. "Crops," which is short for "cropping" printed images, became well-known occasions for scrappers. Stores and organizations that promote drugs would host these plants on a regular basis in order to reach their target demographic and market their products.

Here are some fascinating scrapbooking statistics derived entirely from The National Survey of Scrapbooking in America (2004):

The bulk of fans have been females aged 30 to 50.

Almost half of scrapbookers worked full-time.

82% of scrapbookers were college graduates.

76% of respondents have a separate residence for making duties in their households.

51% of scrapbookers said they scrapbooked at least 10 hours each month.

- Scrapbooking in the Digital Age

Scrapbooking, like modern photography, has grown and flourished as a multi-billion dollar industry as a result of the Internet's upward thrust. Searching for scrapbook elements on the internet is today a piece of cake, especially with the ever-expanding number of scrapbook websites and traditional scrapbook businesses springing up every year. Keeping Memories Alive opened the path for other businesses including Creative Memories Scrapbook Store, Making Memories, and Stampin' Up!, as well as Close to My Heart. Similarly, crafting stores like Altenew have started providing scrapbook paper, scrapbook kits, scrapbooking stamps, and other scrapbooking supplies to cater to the growing number of scrappers. This gained notoriety as soon as non-public curiosity reached scrapbookers in far-flung places, all thanks to the power of the

Internet. Scrapbookers can now easily download free digital layouts or templates that they can print at home. Stickers, wood veneers, journaling cards, washi tapes, reduction files, die-cuts, and other embellishments are now available to enthusiasts, making this hobby more accessible than ever.

Scrapbooking's popularity has also grown as a result of social media. Instagram, Facebook, and Pinterest are excellent platforms for scrapbookers to display their creations and inspirations.

Is Scrapbooking Still Beneficial?

While still popular, the obsession has actually diminished since its peak in the mid-2000s. There were thousands of brick-and-mortar hobby stores dedicated only to scrapbooking equipment and products back then. Retreats and workshops, as previously indicated, have also grown in popularity. These were fantastic activities where scrappers could get together and work on their albums together. Occasionally, instructors would be invited to demonstrate new techniques.

These one-of-a-kind shops and expensive events are less common nowadays, but the interest itself remains popular.

It has just been adapted really well in the digital era. You may no longer be able to attend retreats to share your work, but you can do it through social media. There are still a plethora of scrapbooking websites that provide step-by-step instructions on how to embellish a scrapbook album. While there are less brick-and-mortar retail shops for scrappers, there are now several on-line scrapbook shops where you can get craft materials like customized scrapbook sheets, scrapbook markers, or personalized stickers and have them sent straight to your home.

Furthermore, with its wide range of health and lifestyle benefits, this popular enthusiasm is unlikely to fade away. In fact, in the following part, we'll look at some of the benefits you can get from making your own scrapbook.

CHAPTER TWO

What Exactly Is A Scrapbook?

According to Dictionary.com, a "scrapbook" is a book containing blank pages for putting clippings, drawings, or photographs. Wikipedia, on the other hand, defines it as "a method of preserving, presenting, and arranging personal and household records in the form of a book, box, or card." Photographs, written media, and artwork are examples of common mementos. Albums are frequently embellished and may include extensive journal entries or textual descriptions."

In summary, a scrapbook album is a collection of pages, similar to a book or an image album, that contain images, journaling, ephemera, clippings, letters, tiny trinkets, and various keepsakes. It is typically embellished with stickers, die-cuts, stamped images, colorful washi tapes, journaling, doodling, and other embellishments. Its primary goal is to inform a tale with each page. Here are some of the reasons why people take up the hobby:

To preserve precious memories for future generations.

To celebrate a one-of-a-kind event.

To mark the anniversary of an event.

To truly consider a nice day or an amusing and unforgettable event that occurred on that day.

Take their journaling to the next level.

To practice and hone their crafting skills and techniques such as stamping, alcohol marker coloring, water coloring, mixed media art, and so on.

It's an amazing method to express creativity without putting in too much work.

It's a simple yet effective method of ignoring the passage of time.

Before you begin working on your project, it is critical to research the materials, tools, and components you will need.

The Advantages Of Scrapbooking

There are numerous benefits to creating a personalized album. Here are a few examples that most scrappers can attest to:

For the Preservation of Memories. Do you have a particularly memorable match that you'd like to save in a photo album? You may jazz it up by making it into a scrapbook! To spice up your images, add cute bespoke scrapbook stickers, sweet anecdotes, and collectibles.

Enhances Creativity. The more albums you create, the better you'll become at layouting, design, and color theory. Don't be dismayed if your first attempt isn't as successful as others. It's all about trial and error to see what works and what doesn't. Don't be afraid to challenge yourself. If you're low on scrapbook and creative equipment, see what you can create with a simple pair of scissors and unusual scrapbook papers.

Therapeutic. Creating an album can be beneficial in more ways than one. It might reduce your stress and anxiety levels merely by assisting you to take your mind off things for a bit. Add some soothing music and some healing foods to the mix, and you'll undoubtedly feel at ease while working on your assignment.

Socialization. It may not be as well-known as it once was, but there are still several that hold retreats. Sign up for one if you prefer to work on your project with other scrappers. Of course, you can also collaborate with your friends and family. After all, it's a

unique method to reflect on
historical events.

CHAPTER THEEE

Scrapbooking Tools And Supplies

When it comes to scrapbooking for beginners, it's easy to become overwhelmed by the variety of materials available in local stores and online. It's important to remember that you only need a few components at initially, especially if you're just starting off with this activity.

The Most Important And Primary Materials You Should Have In Your Crafting Supplies.

- Cardstock

Cardstock is a heavyweight paper that is a must-have for any paper crafting hobby. Scrapbook cardstock paper is typically available in bright colors such as white, black, and cream. However, there are more vibrant colors available. Cardstock is frequently utilized as the background of your pages, to matte images, or to highlight specific designs and elements of your page. To ensure that the paper does not turn yellow and lasts as long as possible, choose acid-free and lignin-free sheets. Choosing a long-lasting and durable paper can also protect your images and pages from damage.

- Paper

Just like cardstock, great paper is required for your pages. Patterned paper is a popular choice since it contains a variety of designs, typically in shapes and patterns. Patterned paper is thicker and sturdier than regular printer paper, but not as thick as cardstock paper. They are available in a variety of sizes, colors, weights, and designs.

- Here Are A Few Things To Consider When Purchasing

And Using Scrapbook Paper Packs

Choose graphics that complement your album's overall theme or look.

Single-sided or double-sided paper pads are available. It's better to go with double-sided pads like these Altenew ones.

Size does matter! The majority of patterned sheets are 12" x 12" or 6" x 6". Make certain you understand which size is appropriate for your scrapbook album. Altenew paper packs are available in packs of 12 or sixteen, as well as full bundles like these.

Decorative papers with patterns can be used as gildings or as a background. The beautiful patterns and designs on each paper can be cut out and utilized as ornamental elements on a page.

Reuse, repurpose, repurpose! There's a reason why the word "scrap" appears in the word "scrapbook." Never be afraid to reuse these paper scraps! You can use them as an adornment or even to make confetti.

- Adhesives

The most important thing to remember when purchasing adhesives is that the stickier, the better. Choose from liquid glue, tape runner, glue dots, glue stick, or glue pen. Because scrapbook books are meant to last a long time, it's critical to understand which adhesives can withstand the test of time. Scrapbookers frequently utilize double-sided adhesives and repositionable adhesives because they are high-quality, convenient, and non-messy. Photo-mounting adhesives are also available if you want to ensure that your prized photographs are protected and not damaged. Foam tapes, such as foam squares or foam dots, are perfect for adding dimension.

- Embellishments

You may just as easily make a photo album without any frills. Scrapbook gildings are desired to bring character and uniqueness to your layouts. There are numerous scrapbook embellishments to choose from, ranging from stickers and washi tapes to chipboard frames and die-cuts. You don't have to buy all of them; you may make your scrapbook page stand out with just a few embellishments. These scrapbooking needs can be found in any arts and crafts store, and they are commonly available in ready-to-use units or packs.

Consider the following often used scrapbook embellishments:

Stickers made of chipboard

Alphabet decals

Word decals

Stickers with themes or ornaments

Cards for keeping a journal

Dotted enamel

Frames with embossed foil

Tags

Die-cuts

Ephemera

Innovative cut-outs

The washi tape

Die-cut acetate

Ribbon

Thread made of metal

Lace

Veneer wood

Beads

Buttons made of epoxies

Sequins

Trimmers or Scissors

This is remarkably self-explanatory. If there is paper, you almost certainly need a pair of scissors, trimmers, or some type of cutter. Paper trimmers are well-known among scrappers due to their importance in scrapbooking. If you're looking for a high-quality paper trimmer, Fiskars has a suitable line of paper trimmers that will fit your budget. The most important thing to remember while choosing scissors is to invest in a reputable and excellent one without breaking the money. Titanium precision scissors with ergonomic handles made of stainless steel are the ultimate scrapbooking tool.

Binding versus Album

Unless you've already sold a ready-to-use album, you'll need to figure out how to bind your pages. A D-ring or three-ring binder album is the most common way to collect your pages. This has top-loading web page protectors, which makes inserting, removing, or going around pages easier. Some post-bound books include web page protectors, whereas others do not. The web page protectors would have to be purchased separately.

The three-ring binder kind is the most affordable album type, according to Crafts For All Seasons. The pages in this album can be made from standard acid-free photo-safe sheet protectors. Then slide your completed pages into the protective sleeves. One disadvantage is that you may have a two-page design with a hole where the rings should be, thus the design will not be seamless. If you want a nearly seamless two-page layout, you can go with post-bound albums with top-loading pages. There are also bespoke type books with non-removable pages; however, these frequently lack sheet protectors. You may honestly put your photographs and elaborations onto the page using this type. This is good if your embellishments are thicker. You can then add envelopes or tags that pull out with additional journaling or images.

If you prefer to do more of your own crafting, you can usually make your own album with a paper puncher, some rings, ribbons, or any form of thread. You can also try the well-known "stack the deck binding technique," in which you adhere sections of folded cardstock together to form the cover.

- Scrapbooking Pencils

Having a couple good journaling pens on hand is essential for your scrapbooking experience. If all you need is to write down important dates, names, or brief journaling entries, a black or blue extraordinary factor pen will suffice. You don't want to go overboard with your pens, but you do want to make sure you pick a good one. You don't want to run out of ink while you're writing. Purchasing pens and markers with water-resistant, acid-free, and fade-resistant inks is also vital for longevity. Gel pens are easy to find if you want to add some shine or cute and colorful drawings to your pages. Fine-tipped alcohol marker pens are also ideal if you want to add some calligraphy-like style to your journaling.

If you want to take your scrapbooking abilities to the next level, here are some non-obligatory scrapbook supplies to add to your shopping list.

Page dividers

Sets of stamps and dies

Inks for dyeing

Set of watercolor paints

Brushes (for painting and other mixed media techniques)

Scrapbook paper organization

CHAPTER FOUR

Types Of Scrapbook

As scrapbooking evolved beyond collecting "scrap worthy" scraps to remembering specific events and people through image scrapbooks, unique types of scrapbooks emerged. Here are the eight most common types of scrapbooks.

- Scrapbooking in the traditional sense

This type is typically a collection of pages inserted into page protectors and assembled into a post-bound scrapbook album. A standard scrapbook should be 12" x 12" or 8.5" x 11" in size and contain the standard - photographs, ephemera, and journaling.

- Life of the Project

This is a contemporary type that Becky Higgins started. All you need to do in this simpler version is insert images and writing playing cards into pocketed pages of your scrapbook album. Of course, you can write stories or whatever you want on your journaling cards. To make things easier, you can scrapbook on the move digitally using the Project Life app! This is great for busy bees who want to provide a help with pocket scrapbooking but don't have all the necessary tools.

- Scrapbooking in a planner

What comes to mind when you think of a planner? Is it a leather-bound pocket book stuffed with pages of to-do lists, meetings, reminders, and tedious business notes on a daily, weekly, and monthly basis? Or is it the newest and most renowned Starbucks planner, which you'll get for free after collecting a certain number of "stickers" each time you order a drink? Planner scrapbooking is the process of transforming your unmistakable and simple planner into something more creative and customized. To make your planner more exciting, you can add stickers, stamps, and various souvenirs.

- Scrapbooking in Your Pocket

Pocket scrapbooking is a type of Project Life. Ordinary pocket scrapbooking, on the other hand, necessitates a greater level of engagement and work from the scrapper. Unlike how it has previously been done, this type is significantly simpler because you do not need to graph an entire layout. You only want images, journaling cards, and a few embellishments tucked into pocket pages of your album. Simple as that!

- The Traveler's Journal

A traveler's pocket book is just a leather-bound notebook. The company known as "Traveler's Company" began creating these simple and long-lasting leather-based notebooks, which were a success with both vacationers and craftsmen. A traveler's notebook, according to Bette Ha, is "a piece of leather-based reduce to size, with an elastic strung thru the middle, allowing you to slip a pocket book in between." Another elastic closes the leather and protects the pocket book's contents." In summary, it's a refillable notebook! Enthusiasts have already gone on board and begun adorning their traveler's pocket book with stamps, stickers, ephemera, and various DIY scrapbook accessories. This traveler's pocket book small kit by popular scrapbooker Amy Tangerine is a must-have!

- Journaling in the Bible

Believe it or not, there is a community of creative and non-secular humans who have combined their passion for journaling and trust and developed it into a delightful activity. This style was thought to have begun in the 1400s, but Shanna Noel launched Illustrated Faith in 2014, ushering in modern-day bible journaling as we know it today. While some people embellish their bibles, others like to jot down their favorite bible verses or notes from their bible study on a separate pocket book and embellish it with elaborations and designs.

- Scrapbooking (Digital and Hybrid)

One of the most recent types of inventive scrapbooking, it is obviously capable of creating a sketch or web page on a computer and printing it out. It's a lot like traditional scrapbooking, but without the physical layers, paper slicing, and accessory gluing. Hybrid scrapbooking, on the other hand, is completed by merging some digital and traditional elements.

- Miniature Albums

Mini albums, as the name implies, are quite similar to small picture albums but with more ornamental components, making them a must-try for scrapbookers. Mini albums allow you to focus on a single event, occasion, or theme. It should be about a person, a location, or food. With this style of artwork, the only limit is your imagination.

THE END

Printed in Dunstable, United Kingdom

67138034R00030